RECOLLECTIONS OF JOINING THE EU
IBERIAN AND NORDIC EXPERIENCES

Alan Granadino,
Peter Stadius
& Carl Marklund (eds.)

Södertörns högskola

Institute of Contemporary History
Södertörn University
SE-141 89 Huddinge

shi@sh.se
www.sh.se/shi

Cover image: Street scene, Barcelona.
Photo: Per Lindblom
Cover: Jonathan Robson
Graphic form: Per Lindblom & Jonathan Robson
Stockholm 2023

Samtidshistoriska frågor nr 44
ISSN: 1650-450X
ISBN: 978-91-89615-44-1

Contents

Introduction

Since the 2010s, the statement that the European project is in crisis has become commonplace. The lack of intra-European solidarity during the Euro crisis and the migrant and refugee crises of 2015, the subsequent growing divide between the North and the South of the continent, the emergence of Eurosceptic populist parties as well as Brexit have fuelled this belief. On the other hand, the recent experiences of the coronavirus pandemic and the war in Ukraine have shown that achieving a greater European integration is still feasible. This proves that European integration, as any historical phenomenon, is subject to unexpected changes and that it is not historically determined. The recent crises and uncertainties of the European Union (EU) contrast with the laudatory official narrative on the history of the European integration. This narrative basically consists in considering that in the second half of the 20th century Europeans started to build a union of equal nation-states that agreed on shared rules and institutions, achieving permanent peace and development in the continent. The positive results of this union led to a peaceful, solidary, free, and united continent.[1]

Scholars such as Kiran Klaus Patel have argued that the EU's self-image is exaggerated, and this fact is exacerbating the contemporary perception of crisis.[2] As the EU historical narrative is selective, the problems that we perceive today in the EU seem to be exceptional and unusually dangerous. In fact, European integration has been fraught with danger and encountered a

---

[1] Gilbert, Mark, "Narrating the Process: Questioning the Progressive Story of European Integration," *Journal of Common Market Studies*, Vol. 46, No. 3 (2008), pp. 641–662.

[2] Patel, Kiran Klaus, *Project Europe* (Cambridge: Cambridge University Press, 2020).

variety of different crises since its inception. Therefore, we need a more grounded knowledge of the history of integration in order to contribute towards a more balanced historical narrative that also acknowledges problems, drawbacks, exclusions, concessions, etc. In the last decades, historians have been trying to address this issue by defining new fields of research and by using new methods and analytical approaches.[3] They have applied comparative and transnational history to European integration,[4] focused on initiatives that have been neglected for not having been successful,[5] or framed the history of the EU within global history.[6] The development of the historiography dealing with the EU has been substantial, but the impact of the official European narrative is still important in shaping the national narratives of the countries that joined the EU after the "core six" funding members. When these countries joined the European Communities (EC)/EU, they were entering in a community that stands for peace, freedom, prosperity and integration.

---

[3] See Kaiser, Wolfram & Varsori, Antonio (eds.), *European Union History: Themes and Debates* (Basingstoke: Palgrave Macmillan, 2010); Patel, Kiran Klaus, "Widening and Deepening? Recent Advances in European Integration History," *Neue Politische Literatur*, 64 (2019), pp. 327–357; D'Ottavio, Gabriele, "Disenchantment and new heuristic challenges in European Integration history," *Contemporanea. Rivista di Storia dell '800 e dell '900*, Vol. 23, No. 1 (2020), pp. 99–132.

[4] Loth, Wilfred, *Experiencing Europe. 50 Years of European Construction. 1957–2007* (Baden Baden: Nomos, 2009); Kaiser, Wolfram & McMahon, Richard (eds), *Transnational actors and Stories of European Integration. Clash of Narratives* (Abingdon and New York: Routledge, 2019).

[5] Andry, Aurélie, *Social Europe. The Road Not Taken. The Left and European Integration in the long 1970s* (Oxford: Oxford University Press, 2022).

[6] Hansen, Peo & Jonsson, Stefan, *Eurafrica. The Untold History of European Integration and Colonialism* (London: Bloomsbury Academic, 2014); Warlouzet, Laurent, *Governing Europe in a Globalizing World. Neoliberalism and its Alternatives following the 1973 Oil Crisis* (London: Routledge, 2018); Krotz, Ulrich, Patel, Klaus Kiran & Romero, Federico (eds), *Europe's Cold War Relations. The EC Towards a Global Role* (London: Bloomsbury, 2019); Leucht, Brigitte, Seidel, Katja & Warlouzet, Laurent (eds), *Reinventing Europe. The History of the European Union, 1945 to the Present* (London: Bloomsbury, 2023).

If we take as an example the case of the Iberian countries, the European narrative had an important influence in the redefinition of the Spanish and Portuguese national projects after Franco and Salazar dictatorships. Europe became the symbol of a new Iberian identity, and a catalyst of the expectations of modernization opened by the political change.[7] After their integration, Spain especially became a success story that confirmed the narrative of the European Union as promoter of democracy, freedom and economic as well as social development.

Today, many things have changed in the idealised relation between Europe and the Iberian countries, however. There is still a wide consensus in considering that the overall balance of the European integration has been positive for Spain and Portugal in economic, social and political terms, but structural problems linked to their integration have also been manifested. This invites to enquire further into the EC Southern European enlargement. As recent research has shown, the negotiations for EC integration were not easy for these countries (1977–1986). Integration entailed concessions and sacrifices in the realms of economic and international policy that only now start to be considered by scholars.[8] Furthermore, if it is true that EC integration put an end to centuries of poor bilateral relations between Spain and Portugal, during the process of negotiation with the EC the Portuguese strategy was based on the idea that maintaining the disconnection between both countries would be profitable for Portugal. Portuguese politicians and officials believed that by marginalizing Spain their country could get a better and a faster deal with the Communities.[9] We know very little about the

---

[7] Moreno Juste, Antonio, "El relato europeo de España: de la transición democrática a la gran recesión," *Ayer. Revista de Historia Contemporánea*, Vol. 117, No. 1 (2020), pp. 21–45.

[8] Moreno Juste, Antonio & Sanz, Carlos (eds), *Spain and Portugal before the Second Enlargement of the European Communities. A Comparative Study (1974–1986)* (Basingstoke: Palgrave Macmillan, forthcoming).

[9] Cavallaro, Maria Elena & Muñoz Sánchez, Antonio, "Relações Portugal-Espanha," in Alice Cunha (ed.), *Os Capítulos da Adesão* (Lisbon: Assembleia da República, 2017), pp. 397–410.

Spanish position vis-à-vis its Iberian neighbour, however. This shows a picture that is far from idyllic and suggests that revisiting the history of the Iberian integration into the EC is worthwhile.

For their part, the Nordic countries today seem thoroughly "Europeanized," but the 1990s witnessed a rejection of the Maastricht treaty in a Danish referendum in 1992, slim majorities in favour of EU accession in the Finnish and Swedish referenda of 1994 (as well as a rejection in Norway).[10] Furthermore, contrary to the Iberian idealisation of Europe, among the Nordic countries there were widespread, long-standing concerns regarding the difficulties of conciliating EU membership with Nordic political culture, socio-economic organisation, and international profile. These countries had a strong tradition of international cooperation in the Nordic Council, and historians have subsequently analysed the effects that EU integration had for Nordic cooperation.[11] But, even before that, Finland and Sweden failed to cooperate when they applied to become members of the EC.[12] Therefore, it would be interesting to know more about how the EU integration was foreseen, planned, negotiated, understood and how it came about in both Sweden and Finland. To what extent was there a Nordic coordination of strategies and negotiations with the EU? The personal perspective of key Nordic actors involved in these events is crucial as a starting point for a scholarly reassessment of these events, and valuable by itself as a document of the subjective accounts of some of the key actors involved in this historically significant process.

---

[10] In Finland 56,9% voted in favor and 43,1 % against. Turnout was 74%. In Sweden 52,3% voted in favor and 46,8% against. Turnout here was 83,3%. Kaiser, Wolfram, *"The EU Referenda in Austria, Finland, Sweden and Norway," Unpublished paper, presented at the* 4th *European Union Studies Association (EUSA) Biennial Conference 1995, May 11–14, 1995.*

[11] Strang, Johan (ed.), *Nordic Cooperation. A European Region in Transition* (London: Routledge, 2015).

[12] Uutela, Marjo, "Closer to Germany than Sweden. Finland's way towards the membership application for the EC 1990–1992," *International History Review,* Vol. 42, No. 5 (2020), pp. 1067–1080.

With this witness seminar we aim to widen our knowledge on the processes of European integration in Southern and Northern Europe. We are interested in learning more about the negotiations for EC/EU integration, about the expectations and the realities of integration and about the similarities and differences between the Northern and Southern European experiences. With these objectives in mind, we brought together three relevant political actors that were involved in these historical events: Esko Aho (Finland), Mats Hellström (Sweden) and Juan Antonio Yáñez-Barnuevo (Spain). We consider that the comparison between these cases and the contribution of the oral testimonies of our guests are of critical importance for generating new knowledge and for making this historical source available for future research.

The witness seminar was organized in January 2021, when the coronavirus pandemic did not allow us to travel freely and to have meetings with numerous people. Therefore, this was a hybrid event in which two members of the research team, Johan Strang and Matilda af Hällström, met in person with one of the witnesses, Esko Aho, and online with the other two witnesses, Juan Antonio Yañez-Barnuevo and Mats Hellström.

Alan Granadino, Complutense University of Madrid
Peter Stadius, University of Helsinki
Carl Marklund, Södertörn University

Participants

Researchers

Johan Strang, Professor, University of Helsinki

Matilda af Hällström, Doctoral researcher, University of Helsinki

Witnesses

Esko Aho, Finnish politician, he was the chairman of the Center Party from 1990 to 2002 and Prime Minister of Finland from 1991 to 1995. Under his mandate Finland was integrated in the European Union.

Mats Hellström, Swedish social democrat politician with a long experience in government. He has been Minister of Foreign Trade twice, from 1983 to 1986 and from 1994 to 1996. He was also Minister of Agriculture from 1986 to 1991.

Juan Antonio Yañez-Barnuevo, Spanish diplomat. From 1982 to 1991 he was Director of the International Department of the Cabinet of the Presidency of the Government and he was the diplomatic advisor of the Spanish President Felipe González.

Abbreviations

EC	European Communities
EEA	European Economic Area
EEC	European Economic Community
EFTA	European Free Trade Association
EU	European Union
GATT	General Agreement on Tariffs and Trade
LRF	Lantbrukarnas Riksförbund
NATO	North Atlantic Treaty Organization
NOS-HS	Joint Committee for Nordic research councils in the Humanities and Social Sciences
ReNEW	Reimagining Norden in an Evolving World
UN	United Nations
US	United States

Witness Seminar

Johan Strang

Hello and welcome everyone to this witness seminar titled *Recollections of Joining the EU, Iberian and Nordic Perspectives*. My name is Johan Strang, and I will together with Matilda af Hällström act as the moderator of this seminar. Matilda is the one with European experience, she has worked as the Nordic Council's office in Brussels. And now she is a Secretary of International Affairs at the National Coalition party, but also a doctoral student with us at the Center for Nordic studies, where I work as an associate professor and Academy of Finland research fellow.

Together, we will guide you through this discussion on two different EU accession processes, the Iberian one in the late seventies and early eighties, which led Spain and Portugal joining the European Community from 1986 and the Nordic one, which led to Finland and Sweden joining the European Union from 1995 with Norway rejecting membership, in a national referendum for the second time.

Why is this an important and interesting theme? Today perhaps the most apparent crisis of an established democracy is located outside of Europe, but as Europeans, we have little reason to bask in self-confidence during recent decades, it has become a commonplace to argue that the European project is in a crisis. Great Britain has left the Union. Nationalism is growing across the continent and the refugee and debt crisis have increased the tensions between not only but perhaps particularly the North and South in Europe.

So, the basic idea of this seminar is to look at the processes when the countries in the South and the North joined the European integration project in order to see whether we can identify some differences or similarities in the countries' perceptions of Europe. What were the expectations when joining, what were the key issues in the negotiations and how did the European peripheries conceive of each other during this time? In order to address these questions, we have received funding from NOS-HS, the joint committee for Nordic research councils in the humanities and social sciences, in order to arrange a series of Witness seminars. The seminar is also closely connected to the Nordforsk sponsored university hub, ReNEW, and with my own Academy of Finland project, a research fellowship project called Norden since the End of History. Witness seminar is a form of oral history where scholars discuss with historical actors in a public seminar with the aim of testing ideas and hypothesis in order to get inspiration for new ideas and further research, but also with the intention of creating new source material for future historical research. Our friends and colleagues at Södertörn University who are probably with us online today, have a long tradition of arranging witness seminars, and we are happy to rely on their expertise and knowledge. They are collaborating with us, and we are very thankful for that.

Ideally a witness seminar takes place in a seminar room without masks with witnesses fluently interacting with each other, discussing the topic at lunch and dinner and so forth. Circumstances are what they are and therefore we have, after several postponements, resorted to this hybrid event form. This makes the seminar a bit different, but I'm sure we all have gained enough experience of these forms of seminars in order to manage this as well.

The schedule is simple. We will advance chronologically in three different phases from the pre-accession, motives and visions of Europe to the negotiation processes and further to the North South tensions in Europe. And then we will end by taking some questions from social media, from Facebook. I have been asked by the technical staff to emphasize that it's of utmost importance that we speak only one at the time. And that is my introduction. Matilda, would you care to present our distinguished panel?

Matilda af Hällström

Absolutely, and welcome also on my behalf, we have an excellent set of speakers today. One here in Helsinki, one in Sweden, and one in Spain.

Next to me, we have Mr. Esko Aho who is a former Finnish Prime Minister from 1991 to 1995 and was also a member of Parliament for around 20 years, and longstanding chair for the Center Party in Finland. And because this is a witness seminar, I am also going to ask you a question about what your role was. And since I just already told your role, I'm going to ask a question because we know you as a Prime Minister, you being here today takes a lot of time, but at your time as Prime Minister, how many times did you travel to Brussels?

Esko Aho

I made my first visit to Brussels in October 1991. And between 1991 and 1995, late 1991 and 1995 I visited Brussels, maybe three times a year, something like that. So, total figure is close to ten.

Matilda af Hällström

Which sounds like not so many times.

Esko Aho

I have to say it is a reasonable number. You were busy with domestic politics as well.

Esko Aho

At the time I had a lot of challenges, but 1993, when we were, or actually 1992 probably it was, when we applied for membership, I looked at my calendar afterwards and I visited 29 different countries that year.

Matilda af Hällström

Very impressive.

Esko Aho

In the middle of economic crisis, it was quite a task.

Matilda af Hällström

Then our second distinguished speaker with us from Sweden is Mats Hellström. He is also a former minister in Sweden representing the social democratic party, he was a Minister for Foreign Trade from 1983 to 1986, Minister for Agriculture from 1986 to 1991, and Minister for Foreign Trade again from 1994 to 1996.

Considering, Mats, you were minister up until 1991 and then again from October 1994, there were some critical years that you were outside of government. So, what was your role in these years that you weren't holding a minister post?

Mats Hellström

I was social democratic representative in the negotiation team. That was of course governed by prime minister Carl Bildt,[1] and Frank Belfrage for example, chief negotiator for foreign trade. But in this context, perhaps more important: EFTA. EFTA has not been mentioned in your background, I think that the role of EFTA for Finland, Sweden, and Austria was very important.

I have lots of contacts from my own time as a minister during these negotiations also.

Matilda af Hällström

Thank you very much Mats. And then our final, very distinguished speaker we have all the way from Southern Europe, from Spain, Mr. Juan Antonio Yáñez-Barnuevo – I hope I pronounced your name right – who was a Spanish ambassador and diplomat. And between 1982 and 1991, he was head of the International Department of the Prime Minister's office and a diplomatic advisor to the president Felipe González. And he later went on to become a Spanish permanent representative to the UN and secretary of States on foreign affairs.

---

[1] Carl Bildt was the Prime Minister of Sweden from 1991 to 1994. He was member of the Moderate Party.

You were mainly then in an advisory role during the Spanish negotiations. What exactly does this mean? What were you doing during these negotiations?

Juan Antonio Yáñez-Barnuevo
Good morning, answering your question I would say that I had basically three roles, first at the request of the Prime Minister our office devised a strategy to relaunch the negotiations with the then European Community, which were practically stopped at that time. Second, I had coordination meetings of the different ministries involved, not just foreign affairs, but also economy, commerce, agriculture, etc. to coordinate positions for the negotiations, and third, and most importantly, I accompanied the prime minister in many high-level meetings, in different capitals, Paris, Bonn, London, Rome, you name it, in order to push for a Spanish entry into the European Community.

I will stress that third part because of the way negotiation proceeded. One thing was the technical negotiation in Brussels, but the political accompaniment of all that was, I think, even more important.

Matilda af Hällström
Thank you very much. We shall now go over to the first theme, and I will pass the floor to Johan.

Johan Strang
Yes, thank you. So, the first general theme we would like to address are the visions of Europe or European cooperation, the European Union, European Community, before joining the club, so to speak. What did Europe represent and why was it important to join? What was the general support for joining the Community or Union and what were the defining factors? And the reason why we want to raise this question from a North-South perspective is that it is our hunch that Europe represented very different things from an Iberian, Spanish perspective than from a Nordic perspective. For Spain, perhaps joining Europe was a matter of de-

finitively leaving the authoritarian Franco regime behind and joining democratic European modernity or something like that. From a Nordic perspective, the situation was perhaps a bit different, where Europeanization for some even was perceived as a threat to local or national Nordic traditions of democratic and welfare exceptionality. But starting chronologically with you, Mr. Yáñez-Barnuevo, what did Europe represent and how did the past influence you? From a Portuguese perspective there were past experiences of European cooperation, but Spain did not have that. So, what is your reflection regarding this general topic, what did Europe represent?

Juan Antonio Yáñez-Barnuevo
I think you put the question very clearly and to the point, not just for Spain, I think also for Portugal and for Greece, which preceded both of us in joining the European Community. It was basically a political question. That is to say, it meant to reinforce, consolidate the democracy that we had reconquered with great difficulty, after a long period of dictatorship. Second, to modernize the country, and opening it to the world. So, apart from economic and social considerations, that also existed, it was basically a political project, and it was a project that was shared by the whole political spectrum at the time. It was a consensus strategy, and in the end the ratification of the treaty of accession was attained in parliament by unanimity. I think it was the first time that such a thing happened in the European Community.

Matilda af Hällström
Thank you very much. And I will go on from there, because like Johan earlier said, the perspective from the Nordic countries was quite different when discussing potential membership in the EU. And my question to Mr. Mats Hellström is, if membership in Europe or the EU, or the EEC, from a Spanish perspective was seen as a kind of a step forward to opening up to the world and this whole being tied to democracy, the story looks so different from the Swedish perspective, or does it? Because Sweden had

made a name for itself through a kind of norm entrepreneurship during the Cold War. Sweden exported its values and norms and was quite proud of it as well. So, was EU seen as something that could be made more, let's say, Swedish? Was there a debate at the time about the concessions Sweden had to make when joining the EU and what EU membership meant? Mats, please.

Mats Hellström

I think that you have to go back to the late seventies when in Europe there was a feeling that Europe is lagging behind the development in the United States and Japan, especially. There was also a debate about Eurosclerosis printed by a German resear-cher.[2] The feeling that we were left behind, and that triggered a lot of pain. First, I think in France, when Mitterrand tried to go in his own way with the economic stimulus package for France, it didn't work because he was not connected to the rest of Europe. And that deep thought, I think the finance minister Delors at the time, something that is important, thought that also France had to cooperate with other European nations to be successful at home.

And this happened at the same time while Germany wanted to revive again the European Communities, and you have in the private sector the round table, that was also very much working to see that Europe will go ahead. Then, from this started the White Paper that developed seeing of the markets and there Sweden was very active. We were not just members. We happened to be the chairman of EFTA. I happened to be that during 1984, when Olof Palme made the first and only summit meeting, and we, from the EFTA side, asked the [European] Communities early on about cooperation on a new, single market that will emerge and we were not demandeurs or the cousin from the countryside, but we were very active from the start.

I should not underestimate the role of EFTA in this. Portugal was a very active member of EFTA also. So, the steps to mem-bership in the European Communities and European Union were

---

[2] Mats Hellström is referring to Herbert Giersch, "Eurosclerosis," Kieler Diskussionsbeiträge, No. 112, Institut für Weltwirtschaft (IfW), Kiel (1985).

taken first in the EFTA-EEC cooperation, and then we were certainly active in our country also. That was also giving this understanding that Europe is now moving.

The Swedish government made a government proposition about Sweden's relation with the rest of Europe. I think it was around 1987 or perhaps 1988 when it was said that Sweden would like to cooperate with the Communities in all areas except foreign policy and security policy, of course because of our neutrality. And this last barrier fell down, of course, in 1990, when the Cold War was over and Europe was shaped in quite a new fashion, and that last barrier to Swedish membership went away in 1990, you could say.

So, there was preparation in the political spectrum in Sweden very much that we would like to join European cooperation. And of course, there were differences also within Sweden. For example, within the Social Democrats, my own party, some wanted to go with the European Communities but did not want to give up what was thought of as Swedish social policies for example. So that division within those different parties and the Social Democrats.

Johan Strang

Thank you. This leads us perfectly onto the Finnish case. And I think that for sure, Finland followed the creation of the single market and so forth and was associated to EFTA and so forth. But in terms of visions for Europe during these dramatic years, I guess that the end of the Cold War and the fall of the Soviet Union was of huge importance. At least from a layman perspective, this gave Finland a chance of finally entering the core of Europe or becoming a West European country, or rejoining the family, or something like that. As a historical actor, was this something that you, as Prime Minister, also felt? What were the visions of Europe and what was Finland's role in a future Europe?

Esko Aho

I think it's very important to understand that major political decisions are always made in certain context. Decision-making is contextual, political decision-making is contextual. Sometimes context is rather permanent, and you have rather limited opportunities to make radical changes. And in the Cold War context, I think, like Mats Hellström said, Sweden and Finland had roughly similar interests. We wanted to guarantee free access to the European markets. After EFTA membership, we decided to make free trade agreements with European Community in the early 1970s. That was sufficient – a good solution for Finland and Sweden in those circumstances. And then in the middle of 1980s, Europe started to make radical changes as well. So, it was not only this Eastern context, which was changing but also the Western context.

So, the single market program or single market act was approved, was it 1988? Mats, you probably remember better than me, 86, wasn't it?[3]

Mats Hellström

It was 1987, I think, because Denmark was refusing to take the first step. In late eighties it was approved, and a decision was made and working.

Esko Aho

Yeah, that's right. It was Delors finally, as president of the European Commission, who was able to get through that final plan. And the target was that it will be executed by the end of 1992. And that was a radical change in the context.

So, we had to decide how we can guarantee our position in the market, in those new circumstances and the EEA agreement – the European Economic Area, or the European economic space – was a solution provided for the EFTA countries so that you shouldn't join the Union or the European Community in order to get access to the single market. And that looked as a good solution for us, and we worked hard to get that EEA agreement finalized. Then, quite soon, we recognized that the European Community is going to take steps forward. It wanted to become a European Union and

---

[3] The Single European Act was signed in February 1986, and it came into effect on 1 July 1987.

integration took next steps. And that was changing the position of Nordic countries as well.

And secondly, in our case especially, but also in Sweden's case, the collapse of the Soviet Union led to final phase of the Cold War period. Cold War period was at the end, and the context in that sense changed dramatically as well. It was impossible to imagine that Finland would be able to join the European Communities with the agreement we had with the Soviet Union, we had so-called, agreement on friendship, cooperation, and mutual assistance with the Soviet Union.[4] And it was impossible to imagine that we would be able to apply membership in the Communities with that treaty. And finally, when the Soviet system collapsed, we got rid of that agreement and a new agreement with Russia was signed in January 1992. That opened the door for membership application for Finland as well.

So, I would like to see this contextual change having radical impact in Finland, and Sweden, and Norway as well, Norway applied as well for membership in the European Union, believing that in this way we can in the best way guarantee our economic interests, trade interests, but also political interests in the new Europe that emerged.

Johan Strang

Very shortly a follow-up question. When you talk about "we," it seems that you alter between we-Finland and we-Finland and Sweden and we-Finland and Sweden and Norway. I was thinking about this. This is an obligatory question that we always have to ask when a Finn and a Swede from this period are present in the same seminar. Sweden applied for membership before Finland and some claim even unannounced, or something like that, Koivisto[5] felt betrayed and so forth. Was that something that lingered on during your tenure as a Prime Minister?

---

[4] Between 1948 and 1992 Finland had an Agreement of Friendship, Cooperation and Mutual Assistance with the USSR.

[5] Mauno Koivisto was President of Finland from 1982 to 1994.

Esko Aho

For the first, Mats will be able to explain why the Swedish decision was made exactly in that time. But I understand that it was linked to the internal economic and political situation in Sweden, and application was part of the new policy orientation of the social democratic party. It was a surprise for president Koivisto and the government of Finland. I think a mistake was made maybe in Sweden, but in Finland as well. Message was sent, but it never went through to the leadership of the country, but I didn't see that it had major impact in our relations, I paid an official visit to Sweden. It was a tradition, it is still a tradition, that Finnish Prime Minister is making the first foreign country trip to Sweden. I was there in June 1991, and I think it was very clear that we are going to work together. And when I am speaking about "we," it's quite interesting that in three Nordic countries we had different types of political constellations in all countries after 1991. In Norway, we had social democratic Prime Minister Brundtland,[6] in Sweden we had Carl Bildt, moderate or conservative Prime Minister, and I was representing the Centre Party. Collaboration worked extremely well and that is why I am speaking about "we," because we had a common understanding on how to act and what our targets were.

Some people are able to say that maybe it was just because of that what we represented. We were representing different political orientations. It made it easier to work together than if the leaders have been from the same party affiliation. It is difficult to say, but anyway, collaborations worked well and the word "we" is fitting very well in this context.

Matilda af Hällström

And building further on the word "we," I'm quite interested to hear about the Iberian Peninsula. Was there this kind of "we"-feeling in the negotiations between Spain and Portugal, even though the democratization process had its differences in Spain

---

[6] Gro Harlem Brundtland, she was Prime Minister of Norway in 1981, again from 1986 to 1989, and again from 1990 to 1996.

and in Portugal. Was there this sense of "we," that we just heard, relating to some of the Nordic countries?

Juan Antonio Yáñez-Barnuevo
I think that, in a sense, there is a certain parallelism between the two processes, although in different historical moments. Both Portugal and Spain did it after their respective first democratic elections, in the case of Portugal it was in 1976, in Spain in 1977, so, less than a year's difference. Each of the two countries immediately submitted their candidacy for membership in the European Community. And, also, must I say, for joining the Council of Europe, I think that is very important because the first step for both countries was to join the Council of Europe as the main European institution, regarding human rights, democracy, etc.

So, each of the two countries joined the Council of Europe with little difference, first Portugal, then Spain.[7] And at the same time they presented their candidatures in Brussels. This made Portugal, to a certain extent, wanting to join first. Following the example of Greece, because Greece was granted also that early access. I think it was in 1981,[8] thanks to the goodwill of President Giscard d'Estaing.[9] Portugal and Spain did not get the same green light from Paris, for economic reasons basically, the competition in certain agricultural products, mainly fruits and vegetables. The fact is that for internal political reasons in France, also on the eve of the presidential elections that took place in 1981, Giscard d'Estaing decided to call for a pause in the EEC negotiations with Spain and Portugal.

I think the main reason was Spain, because it was a larger country which presented much more of a threat to French farmers. But they put us in the same bag, Spain and Portugal. So, from 1981 to 1982, 1983, there was a pause in the negotiations that had just started, had only progressed very little in some technical

---

[7] Portugal joined the Council of Europe on 22 September 1976, and Spain in on 24 November 1977.

[8] Greece joined the EC on 1 January 1981.

[9] Valery Giscard d'Estaing was President of France from 1974 to 1981. He was member of the Republican Party.

areas, but the crux of the negotiation will still to be done when Giscard called for that pause.

And then when he lost power in the 1981 election to Mitterrand.[10] Mitterrand for his own reasons continued that policy for some time. So, there was a difficult situation between Spain and France at that time, also for other different reasons relating to the threat from terrorism. As you may remember, some terrorist group was based in Southern France and committing attacks in Spanish territory, it was a separatist group,[11] and from Spain it was felt that France was not doing enough to impede those activities.

In the meantime, there was a change of government in Spain. That was very important. Why? The government that had presented the candidacy to the European Community was a centrist or center-right government, but which was a minority government and very divided in its own ranks. It was a sort of constellation of little political groups and at a given moment that constellation and that government started to crumble. And soon after there was a general election in end of 1982, and there was a government with a large majority, the largest that we have had in the modern democratic history of Spain, in which the socialist government led by Felipe González[12] had an absolute, a large absolute majority in parliament. So, it changed the landscape.

It was a very pro-European government, and it could speak with a strong voice within Spain and towards the rest of Europe, France particularly, also Germany and in Brussels, and this gave a new impulse to the negotiation.

Also, the personal involvement of Felipe González, who knew all the principal actors in Europe, and had very good working

---

[10] François Mitterrand was President of France from 1981 to 1995. He was member of the Socialist Party.

[11] Yañez-Barnuevo is referring to ETA (*Euskadi Ta Askatasuna* – Basque Country and Freedom).

[12] Felipe González was President of the Government of Spain from 1982 to 1996. He was member of the Socialist Party.

relationship with his Portuguese counterpart Mário Soares,[13] also a socialist leader. They knew each other very well, they had a very good personal relationship. One of the first things González did was to get in touch and to have a good coordination with Portugal. Of course, the problems were not exactly the same. And as I said, Portugal, to a certain extent, still aspired to go first, but soon thereafter it was clear that the two processes were somehow linked.

Brussels didn't want to make all the effort to have just Portugal and then one or two, three years later, Spain. It was clear that it had to be the two together.

So, Portugal renounced that early entry and since then we had a very good coordination. Then, there were two separate negotiations with the EEC, but good coordination between us.

Johan Strang

Very good. Let's move on to the second theme. The divisions between the three themes are not set in stone, but they go into each other and so forth. The idea is that the second theme is perhaps the most concrete one and dealing with the negotiation processes themselves, or the period when countries were trying to establish a permanent relationship with Europe. And we are interested in identifying key issues and obstacles in the negotiations, but also bilateral relations during the negotiation, which we have already covered to a certain extent. Which were the most important partners or problematic partners, challenging partners among the EU countries and what was the regional dynamics within the Iberian Peninsula and the Nordic region? Did you help each other or was there cooperation?

Starting with Esko Aho, you were the leader of the center party, the older agrarian league which is not exactly known, or was at that point in time not exactly known, as the most pro-European of the largest parties in Finland. To the contrary, there was a large opposition that you had to deal with. And I have often wondered

---

[13] Mário Soares was Prime Mister of Portugal from 1976 to 1978, and again from 1983 to 1985. He was also President of Portugal from 1986 to 1996. He was member of the Socialist Party.

about the significance for Finland, like in a long-term perspective of having a center party prime minister at this crucial point in time. European Union is a lot about agriculture, did this kind of influence, do you think that there was a difference for example, in comparison to Sweden?

Esko Aho

The starting point in Sweden was in that respect easier when thinking about EU policies, because when you started to negotiate or even when you started to send the application to the European Union or to the Communities, you had to analyze what kind of obstacles you are going to face when negotiations are going to be started. And we made very thorough analyses before making the final decision to apply for membership. And we came to the conclusion that actually, we had three elements in our application. For the first, we expected that EEA agreement is still relevant because we were able to solve most of the problems, most of the challenges facing with membership through that agreement. 80%, 90% of the content is clear when EEA agreement is finalized, that was issue number one. Issue number two was the fact that Nordic, or Northern circumstances were in some areas quite different compared with the existing European Communities and that was especially relevant with agriculture. It was agriculture and food processing. We had high level of protection in our own country, like in Norway as well. So, Finland and Norway were quite close to each other, as far as the agriculture and food processing was concerned. The Swedish situation was a bit easier. Sweden had not that many difficulties to absorb the European Common Agricultural Policy. Our target was that we have to be able to not only change Finland and the Nordic countries when joining the union, but like in the Southern European cases as well, the Union or the Communities or Community has to be changed as well when new members are coming.

So, the question was how the Northern dimension will be integrated into the union policies when Finland, Sweden and Norway will join. That was issue number two. And then issue number three, which was extremely important in spite of the fact that we had some hesitation if that decision would be important or not, but already before application was sent, if I remember correctly in January 1992, two months before decision to apply was made in our parliament, we decided in the government that after the negotiation process there is going to be a referendum. President Koivisto didn't like that idea that much. The chairman of the social democratic opposition party Ulf Sundqvist[14] was against the referendum. But for me, it was extremely important to have that commitment in the beginning, in order to show that we are going to make an open process, a process which is going to lead to the situation that every single Finn has the right to participate in decision-making.

And I am quite confident that that was an extremely important part of the process, that those not that excited about EU membership were able to join this process and agree that this was going to be a process which at the end of the day would be acceptable for all.

Johan Strang
But how did you deal with the opposition within your own party against this?

Esko Aho
I think it was important to respect different opinions, and that was sometimes a problem with those who were extremely excited about the EU membership. Their idea was, why don't we go into the Union and that is it. And to be honest, it was not that simple because we had rather complicated issues to be solved. And then secondly, in order to get those who were against to be in the process, you have to listen to them. You have to take them seriously. You have to meet them face to face.

---

[14] Ulf Sundqvist was Chairman of the Social Democratic Party of Finland from 1991 to 1993. Before that, he served as Minister of Education from 1972 to 1975, and as Minister of Trade and Industry from 1979 to 1981.

I think that is something which has changed in politics today. People are not anymore meeting face to face. They are not anymore listening to different opinions. They are only trying to have people around them who have exactly the same kind of worldview, and that is dangerous.

In the case of this decision-making, we were open to different opinions and I met tens of thousands of people in different parts of the country to discuss, even angry people who were strongly criticizing us. But we met these people face to face. It was an open, democratic, transparent process.

And that was <u>one</u> reason why in Finland since the decision was made, in spite of the fact that more than 40% of people voted against the membership, they never started to fight against the membership anymore. It was over and they accepted the fact that the decision had been made.

Matilda af Hällström
In Norway the situation went the other way because they also had a referendum, where a majority voted to not enter the EU.

Johan Strang
And I am now going to ask Mats Hellström a question about this Norwegian dimension which Esko Aho has very much mentioned already. Because normally when we talk about the Finnish and Swedish accessions it is focused on Finland and Sweden. But sometimes we forget that there were the Norwegian negotiations at the same time as well. And today it is often said that there would be a much stronger Nordic block in the EU if also Norway was a member of the EU. Was there at the time, Mats, a perception that there would be a joint Nordic block in the EU before the Norwegian referendum, and what kind of contacts were kept and maintained with the Nordic counterparts? Esko was already talking about that, on the cooperation between the prime ministers, between different parties, but what kind of contacts were there, and was there the idea of a Nordic block to come?

Mats Hellström

There were a lot of contacts certainly, but do not forget this was an EFTA accession. This is not just the Nordic countries, but also Austria. And there were intense discussions between those countries and the leaderships and sometimes the oppositions. I do not think we ever thought about the Nordic bloc. We were warned rather by the old members that you should not divide the Communities in regional blocks, that could be counter effective. And in fact, you had to find allies in different countries, different situations. And you should not think about a bloc. But that of course does not mean that we were not negotiating, Sweden and Finland especially, I will come back to that.

Ingvar Carlsson,[15] the Swedish prime minister was very careful to see to it that he would inform the Finnish leadership and the Norwegian leadership about the ideas of the Swedish government. That we should ask the first committee in parliament to go into this question about membership. It was not an application, but it was a request to the parliament to go into the EU membership. And he in fact informed both Finland and Norway, but the message did not come through, as Koivisto was in Portugal, not because of the Swedish communication, but somewhere on the Finnish side, it was lost, and he was angry. In fact, Ingvar Carlsson was careful enough to see to it that they informed them of this idea to Norway and Finland, even before it was mentioned to the social democratic group in Swedish parliament. So, I am happy that Esko is not going to this myth, that has been created, that we wanted to go alone, rather it was very parallel.

And certainly, there was a lot of cooperation with the Norwegians and the Finnish. On some issues, Finland and Sweden worked very closely together in the negotiations, especially on the question of the regional support schemes, where we asked that our batted north, *glesbygd* in Swedish, to get the strongest regional support that existed in the European Communities.

---

[15] Ingvar Carlsson was Prime Minister of Sweden from 1986 to 1991 and again from 1994 to 1996. He was member of the Social Democratic Party.

And that was very parallel act between Sweden and Finland. And we succeeded in that. On the other hand, when it comes to agriculture, it was very difficult. Sweden had just – and I happened to serve in the cabinet during that time – made a deregulation of agriculture.

We had very strong drink legislation before that, even worse than the European Communities, but we deregulated, and we wanted the slimmer agricultural support. Whereas Finland wanted to keep that support, and Norway also very much wanted to keep the support.

So, in fact the Swedish farmers, the LRF, they were the main actors in the campaign for membership because they hoped to get back some regulations, that were still there in the European Communities that we had left. On the Norwegian side has been mentioned that in the *Bondelaget*, they were the leading groups for the no-campaign. Because they saw the European Communities support scheme as a threat. So, there are big differences between both our attitudes when it came to agriculture. And, of course, also reflected, I guess, also the regional differences in the counties in Sweden, in Stockholm 60% voted yes, whereas in the Northern Sweden, only one town, Sandviken, voted yes. There was a fairly slim no in the university town Umeå, but otherwise that was clearly a difference between big cities and the countryside.

That was also true in Norway, where Oslo and Bergen voted yes, the countryside voted no. So, these were some important differences. Also, similarities on the *glesbygds*-support, batted north support. To me, that's very important. Then another issue, in Sweden's case it was seen that the environmental support schemes were too weak in the Communities and that we had stronger environmental protections in our country. That was one of the tricky issues in the negotiations. And we managed to find a solution where in fact, we could keep our stronger environmental support schemes. In the perception that when we kept our standards – we had the understanding, or European Communities had the understanding, that European Communities will aspire to reach those levels. So that was one way of solving this.

We also had another issue which was controversial. As Sweden had not been part of the Maastricht negotiations or decisions, we reserved our right to have the Swedish parliament to decide on an eventual participation in the Euro currency. And as you know, we are not members of the Euro currency. It was also a very tricky part of the negotiations. Apart from those, we were helped much, I think by Delors in the commission of course, and by the German government, Helmut Kohl himself and also the foreign minister Klaus Kinkel and also the Belgian presidency of the European Communities at the time,[16] Willy Claes, the foreign minister of Belgium.

We were also very active to support the EFTA countries accession and it went, as you know, very well. We also had a referendum the 13th of November – and that's just after the Swedish parliament elections. When we regained power, I had the privilege of becoming the first EU minister. I know you asked also in your background paper about new visions, I would say that during the negotiations and the preparations for the referendum, I would say that it was a vast important study circle, where we learned a lot about implementing this in a positive way, basically. And I had made the comparison with the implemented elections that we just had, and there were much more sharp divisions and with tougher attitudes perhaps than this study circle on learning about Europe, that was part of our referendum.

Johan Strang

Thank you, moving on to the Spanish or Iberian perspective then, I mean, agriculture was certainly a key theme also in those negotiations. I guess that France, to a certain extent also Italy, were concerned of Spanish and Portuguese competition, but was it all about oranges, olive oil, and wine, or was there other key issues in the negotiations? Fishing industry, Spanish migration, democracy, even police and security cooperation with regard to the terrorism issues that you mentioned previously? So, what were the key factors and which country – was it France? – that was the most important counterpart that you had to convince politically?

---

[16] This probably refers to the Presidency of the Council of the EU.

Juan Antonio Yáñez-Barnuevo

I think we have to separate, as I said before, the issues being discussed at the negotiating table in Brussels between the European Commission and the Spanish delegation, on the one hand, and, on the other, political or security issues that were more of a bilateral kind, as I mentioned, with France or on wider security issues, Europe, Atlantic Alliance, et cetera. I will try to distinguish the two, on the negotiating table you mentioned, agricultural issues, no doubt. In the case of Spain, it was basically the question of access for our agricultural produce, especially Mediterranean products, but let us not forget also we had to open our market for productions, like meat and milk products, etc., or wheat, that were more efficiently produced in France or elsewhere in Europe. So, also, on agriculture, there were different kinds of interests that had to be balanced, basically as regards calendars. How long would be the transition for each chapter or each regime? Because from the start, and I suppose it was the same thing for Nordic countries, it was clear that each candidate had to accept the *acquis communautaire*. That is to say, not just the European treaties, but also the whole secondary legislation and regulation, etc. that European institutions had produced in four decades. But the question was how to graduate, over a period of time, the gradual acceptance in practice, gradual entry into force of those regimes for Spain or for other candidates.

And the other way around as well. Apart from agriculture, fisheries played a very important role because of the large Spanish fishing fleet that had been working for many years in European waters and elsewhere as well. But again, there was also a sort of trade-off because the Spanish market, Spaniards are very fond of fish, also we had to open our markets to imports from other countries.

Anyway, the question of migration, it is curious – or manpower, if you will – was mentioned a lot in the negotiations, but I think it was a concern on the part of our European partners that was misguided. Why? We had a lot of Spanish workers that had gone to other European countries, mainly Germany, France, Belgium and some others in the fifties, sixties and seventies. But, once Spain got into the European Union, there was no migration at all, or very little from 1986 onwards. It was a question of better protecting the rights, the vested rights of those people that were already settled in other countries of the European Community, but there was very little movement, except for businessmen, or students, it was a quite different thing.

Now, I would like to mention not just the matters that were discussed at the negotiating table, but curiously enough, there were other issues, and I was reminded of that by the references you made to the case in Sweden and in Finland of the overall political and security situation following the end of the Cold War. And that, of course was very important for your countries, vis-à-vis the situation in the Soviet Union and then Russia. In our case, it was different, and I will try to explain. The question was NATO. It was a totally different matter from the negotiating table in Brussels.

I wish to stress that this never figured in the negotiation as such, but in a way, it floated around the negotiation and to certain extent became interlinked with it. I will explain. Spain had the tradition since the 19th century of isolation, of not being involved in formal alliances. Spain was, as Sweden too, neutral in the First World War and in the Second World War, in different contexts, of course. But then in 1953, the Franco regime got into a bilateral security relationship with the United States. So, in a way, Spain became linked to Western security and defense arrangements through the back door. Not by the formal entry into the Atlantic Alliance, because Franco was of course considered politically by many NATO countries as not good company. And he understood that very well, of course.

Anyway, the then centrist government, a weak minority government, decided to go ahead with accession to the Washington treaty and entry into NATO in the years 1981, 1982. Now, this was resisted by the left-wing parties, the socialist party and the communist party. For various reasons, I will not go into all the details. The fact is that the parliament was divided, but by a narrow majority, the accession to NATO was approved in parliament with certain conditions.

Anyway, this was the panorama that the socialist government found when acceding to power in Spain at the end of 1982. In the electoral program, in the electoral platform of the socialist party, there were two promises made to the Spanish people. First, to freeze the situation of accession to NATO as it found it when elected. So, it meant no going back, no going forward for the time being. Second, further on to hold a referendum on the question of belonging or not to NATO, without committing one way or the other. Those were the formal promises in writing in the program, but of course, what many citizens felt was that referendum would be a referendum to leave NATO. That was not true, but it was the psychological impression, many got from that.

So, this was the atmosphere during the active period of negotiation of entry into the EEC in 1983, 1984, 1985. That was the key period, and everybody was aware of that. So, the prime minister, in a very skillful way, I must say, in his bilateral contacts with the leaders of other European countries belonging to NATO, mainly, I would say Germany, also Britain, also France, Italy, the Benelux countries, he always maintained, and also publicly, vis-à-vis the Spanish public opinion, a policy of what could be called "calculated ambiguity".

Calculated ambiguity, so, he always stressed that the socialist party and the government would be faithful to what was in the political program, but never openly showing his cards. To be frank, he used that perspective of the referendum. He always said that would be a referendum, but he used that in order to surmount difficulties with other countries, to press for early entry into the European Community. He explained that the Spanish public opinion was very reluctant to maintain that kind of commitment to the common defense. One way to convince the citizenry in Spain would be to show that we were fully accepted into European institutions. On the other hand, he always stressed that there should not be any kind of political pressure vis-à-vis Spain on that matter, but to leave sovereignty to the Spanish people in deciding.

It was, I think, helpful in accelerating the rate of negotiation and the entry of Spain into the European Community. And then he went to the Spanish people, convened the referendum after the Spanish entry in 1986. And then he said, basically the message was, I will say it in Spanish, *hay que estar a las duras y a las maduras*, it is a very colloquial expression, it means in English, I think: "we have to take the rough with the smooth." We have to follow both the rough and the smooth in a path. I mean, we have to take the good and the bad for Spain. Without saying it in so many words, the good was the EEC, the bad was NATO. I mean, for the Spanish people. In the end, he [Felipe González] got what he wanted. The Spanish people backed him by more than 50% of the vote, with 40% against. It was a great personal triumph.

Spain is the only country, I think, that has supported membership of NATO by a referendum. It's very curious, I was thinking of that. We did not hold a referendum regarding entry into the European Community. It was not necessary according to our Constitution, it was just the vote in parliament, which was unanimous.

Matilda af Hällström

Thank you. Thank you very much. I am just going to have a quick comment that Esko asked for. When Mats was speaking, Esko's hand immediately went up when Mats claimed that there was some kind of broken telephone on the Finnish side as opposed to the Norwegian side regarding the Swedish application, what do you have to say?

Esko Aho

I have a couple of comments, first one was about that broken connection. What I have learned is that Tom Westergård[17] who was, I think he was in prime minister Holkeri's[18] office in the previous serving the previous government, when the Swedish

---

[17] Tom Westergård (1935–2009) was a Finnish civil servant. He served as governor of Vaasa County from 1991 to 1997. He was member of the Social Democrat Party. He was close assistant of the President Mauno Koivisto.

[18] Harri Holkeri was Prime Minister of Finland from 1987 to 1991. He was member of the National Coalition Party.

decision was made in summertime, we had summer holidays and Swedish government could not reach, or could not find, Mr. Carlsson could not reach president Koivisto or prime minister Holkeri and a message was sent to Tom Westergård, and for some reasons he did not get that message forward. And that was the broken phone in this case. So, it was a sad story because for sure it had an impact, so that president Koivisto took it very seriously and it had some negative consequences in his mindset. But, as I said, it did not have any impact in the negotiation process itself or in the collaboration between Nordic countries in that process.

Secondly, about Nordic bloc, it is very interesting how the European Communities and European Union is acting, there are sometimes double standards. And one double standard was related to the Nordic bloc. It was forbidden, or they said it is not acceptable that certain member countries are working together and trying to have an influence together. But the fact is that Germany and France are doing that. And many other countries are doing that, but in some way, it was not acceptable as far as the Nordic countries were concerned. And I think we had good reasons to work together. We had common interests, Mats Hellström mentioned the environmental aspect, which was very critical. And when I was at Harvard University, I was listening to one US professor who said that when Finland, Sweden and Austria joined the European Union the fact is that the Union's environmental power and environmental policy influence increased substantially.

But another example of double standard is related to agriculture policy. This key idea required that you have to take the union as it is, or the Communities as they are, you cannot expect that policies will be changed in order to get new countries to join. And as a consequence, we were told that we can join the union or the Communities only with the existing agriculture policy. That was exactly stated. And we could not ask any changes in the agriculture policy in our case. When Central and Eastern European countries joined a bit later in the next round, the same EU commission was saying, you cannot join with the existing agriculture policy. You cannot be accepted if the rules will be the same. So, it is a good example that sometimes there are double standards. But anyway, we had to work together in order to get some changes, which made it possible that these Nordic circumstances will be taken into consideration.

I have couple of practical examples of that, but we can come to those later on.

Johan Strang

Thank you. And then turning to the final theme, time is moving very fast and we want to save something for general discussion, to take some questions from social media as well. But the final theme is more about trying to bring the two cases together and the two peripheries of Europe together. And to talk a bit about North-South relations. So, since the financial crisis in particular, the tensions between North and South in Europe has grown, and the refugee situation has only escalated this. So, historians have analyzed North-South relations often from a longer historical perspective and my colleague Stefan Nygård has edited a brilliant book about this from the perspective of debt.[19] But in the eighties, particularly in the nineties, I guess that North-South was over-shadowed by East-West. So, we are interested in the extent to which there were any particular issues that united or divided the North from the South during this point in time. And how did you view each other's accession processes, and how did cooperation between these peripheries work within the European Union? So, if we can start with perhaps a Spanish perspective Juan Antonio Yáñez-Barnuevo. Members of the European Union, quite estab-lished members or recent members in the European Union, how did you view Finnish, Swedish, Austrian and Norwegian acces-sion negotiations and their final entry to the European Union? Did you feel a sense of affinity, like we're part of the same family, or were there any concerns about Nordic membership? Elderly

---

[19] Johan Strang is referring to Stefan Nygård (ed.), *The Politics of Debt and Europe's Relations with the "South"* (Edinburgh: Edinburgh University Press, 2020).

flooding your healthcare systems or something like that or was it seen as an opportunity for export or something? Was there a fear that Europe would become more German?

Juan Antonio Yáñez-Barnuevo

Well, thank you. I would like first of all, excuse me, to go back a little bit to what was just said by our Finnish colleague, which I found very important. This matter of change or not change of our *acquis communautaire*, because this brings me to the negotiations of Spain and Portugal on the EEC. It is true that the *candidate countries* cannot change what is the existing state of the Community arrangements or legal settings, but of course the *member states* can, and this is what happened also at the time of Spanish and Portuguese accession. The reason why France established that pause in the negotiation was because France wanted to change certain things in the existing agricultural policy, and above all the financing of those policies through the European budget. And there was resistance already then by Germany for that. This was something that they had to settle between them, between France and Germany. And we had to sit and wait, in a way.

So, I remember when we arrived in government and the prime minister asked us to draft a strategy to unblock the negotiation. It was very simple, well it was more complex than that, but we basically said: between Madrid and Brussels, this road has to pass through a door in Paris. And we have to find a way to open that door in Paris and that key was in Bonn. So, we had to both work with the French to mollify them in a way but also, we had to find an ally in Germany, and this is what he did.

Being aware of that, González managed to establish a very good working relationship with Helmut Kohl, even if the two belonged to different parties and different generations, but they worked together fantastically well in order to convince the French to open that door. But of course, the French also got a good part of what they wanted in terms of changes in the agricultural policy and above all in the financing of the EEC budget. But that was key, certainly.

Now, to return to your question, I find it a bit difficult to pronounce myself because at that time I was no longer in Madrid. I was no longer in the prime minister's office. I was then working in New York at the UN and that is quite a separate thing. But my feeling is that from the perspective of two newcomers, like Spain and Portugal, we could not in any way make an obstacle to the entry of new members. On the contrary, we looked at the opening of the European Union with a lot of sympathy and especially for the Nordic countries, with whom we have excellent relations.

I remember that during my time in the prime minister's office Felipe González visited all the Nordic countries, I think, except Iceland. So, he went to Sweden, of course, he had a marvelous personal relationship with Prime minister Olof Palme. I remember very well the personal meetings in the country residence or the Swedish prime ministers in Harpsund, and also in Norway too, with prime minister Brundtland, as well as in Denmark and Finland, he visited all those countries.

So, he was not only centered in the European Community, he wanted also to work with the surrounding countries. And certainly, Spain must have favored also the entry of the Nordic countries, I think, especially because we receive a lot of citizens from the Nordic countries to Spain, be it as tourists or as retirees or as businessmen. And we aspired to receive a lot of foreign investment and technological transfer that we needed. So, I think we did not have much of a difficulty. I think we wanted to ensure, especially regarding Norway, as much access as possible for our fishermen. Again, fisheries, but as Norway in the end did not join the European Community this problem continued to exist, no doubt.

I would say basically our position must have been very positive, except for perhaps certain details. I have perhaps a different idea regarding the enlargement of the EEC to the East but that's another matter. That's another story completely.

Matilda af Hällström
And now Esko, I will ask you, it is a bit of the same question that we just heard here, but the other way around. So, when you were

doing these negotiations, there were some countries that had done them quite recently. During the negotiations, did you look to the cases of Spain and Portugal for best practices or examples, or did you receive any advice? Were you in touch with these representatives of Spain or Portugal or even Greece to kind of learn how to do it?

Esko Aho

Because the time was very different, even though the time between the negotiations was rather short, because we had the fall of the Berlin wall and collapse of the Soviet Union in between. If I remember correctly, we made some studies in the early phase and we tried to analyze the process. But the fact is that the situation in the late 1980s and early 1990s had changed dramatically because of the EA agreement. It was not yet finalized, but we were well positioned in the negotiation table. It was totally different because most of the issues were already settled because of that EA agreement.

So, our obstacles for the membership were much more limited. And that is why I think we could not learn that much from the cases of the Mediterranean countries. The only thing we learned was that every time when the EEC has expanded, every time it has changed as well. When enlargement has taken place, the Union has become a bit different as well. And that happened when the Mediterranean countries joined. So, it was a bit different type of the European Union after that, and we expected that the very same is going to happen also when the Nordic countries will join, when this Northern dimension would be integrated. And I think Helmut Kohl[20] understood this very well. He was playing a critical role in getting the final decision to be made. Without his contribution I think it would have been difficult to get a final political decision to be made on 1st March 1994, this political agreement was made because of strong involvement by the German government.

Mr. Kinkel was there in Brussels personally to promote the final phase. And the reason why Kohl was so strongly in favor of

---

[20] Helmut Kohl was Chancellor of Federal Republic of Germany and, later, unified Germany 1982 to 1998.

expansion of the EEC, the main reason was that he wanted to have better balance inside Europe, so that the Mediterranean accession was important, but that led to a new kind of balance inside the EU, and he wanted to change that balance again. And again, it changed when Central and Eastern European countries joined.

So, that was a relevant part of the process. Finally, when thinking about our negotiation process, in different member countries, to be honest, we had some challenges with existing members.

I want to mention especially Greece, because the fact is that the Greek government and Greece had the approach that when Nordic countries and EFTA countries, Austria as well, when they are going to join, Greece had to get some compensation for that. From our perspective it was a bit crazy idea, why to compensate existing member countries only because of the fact that new entrants are coming in?

But that was the Greek approach, and it created a lot of practical technical difficulties in the negotiation process. Finally, we were able to overcome this, but to be honest, it was a bit frustrating in certain phase, because we recognize that our membership was not blocked, or tried to be blocked because of our policies, our role, but because of the fact that the EU was not able to give enough compensation for existing members.

Johan Strang
So, Finnish-Greek tensions there is prior to that, when thinking about the financial crisis etc. If we turn to Mats Hellström then, you are the one who has government experience from both these accession processes though Sweden was, of course not a member of the European Union when Spain and Portugal joined the EEC, but I would love to hear your reflections both on the Spanish and Portuguese accession to the European Community. And then also, whether that has played any role for Swedish thinking about European cooperation in the eighties, but then also perhaps about your relations, or Swedish relations to Southern Europe during the negotiation processes and early years within the European Union.

Mats Hellström

First, when it comes to the North-South relations. Spain became the presidency, and we had a very good cooperation with Spain, very intense and good. And in fact, transatlantic initiative that started little earlier, was taken over by the Spanish presidency, they did a very good job with that. I worked very much with the secretary of state in Spain then for European affairs, personally, we had just very good relations and cooperation. So, there is no sort of North-South divide thinking, rather of course what was occupying our minds all the time, was how to make it easier for the East European countries to become members, not least of course, the Baltic states, but also the other countries. That was a strong preoccupation from our side.

Secondly, one should not forget that the whole time we were negotiating on membership, that was an ongoing GATT negotiation on deregulating agriculture worldwide. And that was a complicated negotiation. It was finalized, more or less at the same time as we became members of the European Union. And, of course, it led to certain deregulation also in the European agriculture, and the European agriculture has been moving a lot since then.

So, it was not a fixed sort of agriculture package to take but also something that we could work in the GATT round to stimulate the European union or European Communities to move it along also. So that was an important thing. We've tried of course and we were very strongly committed to that round of negotiations, and through that we also influenced somewhat the EEC agriculture moving in a less regulated direction.

So, that is another international sphere where we could work outside of the European Union before we became members and through the whole negotiation process. And on the Iberian exception, we were of course very close to Portugal and we wanted to help Portugal in their negotiations. They wanted to liberalize textile industries that sort of changed a little when they became members of European Communities, but that is of course, another story. And about North-South, which was mentioned in your background talk, I hope, and I think most people hope, that this North-South dividing will be less intense now within enormous pandemic recovery package called next generation EU, where Germany has moved so much from their earlier positions on common financing of European matters. So, I do hope that this one somewhat elevates the skepticism of the countries. Unfortunately, we still have another problem, which is the East-South, Poland and Hungary, and we hope that solutions that have been made now will lead to certain governmental policies. I doubt that it will happen easily, but perhaps liberal Biden leadership in the US will make the Polish government reconsider somewhat that position, but this is just a speculation. Good relations disappeared and perhaps, but I am not sure this could be something where a liberal Biden leadership could somewhat help the Hungarian government to reconsider, but I am not sure.

Matilda af Hällström
Thank you. In your comment you covered already vast period of time from the eighties, nineties, towards the present day. And that gives us the opportunity to move forward to the next item on our timetable, which is questions from our audience.

And for those of you who have, for some reason, stumbled upon this on the internet, without knowing where to put a question, you will find us through the Centre for Nordic Studies homepage, and there you will find this seminar as well, and you can post questions there.

And I believe we already have one question, or at least one, I do not know. We do indeed have one question here and I remind that the question needs to be posted on the Facebook page, even though the stream is on another website, the questions must be posted on the Facebook page.

And we have a very interesting question here, which is addressed to Mr. Esko Aho and Mr. Yáñez-Barnuevo, regarding their experience with their respective territorial autonomies in this case Åland Islands and in the Spanish case the Basque Country and Catalonia, what kind of relationship did you have with these regions during the negotiations and how would you describe your relationship at the time with these regions?

Esko Aho

I visited Åland Islands at least once, maybe a couple of times during that process. We had several meetings in Helsinki in our capital during that process. I think we had a common understanding that these special issues related to Åland Islands have to be taken seriously. And the final agreement we reached was in line with that, so it was an integral part of our process, and it was also one example of what kind of critical issues we had in the negotiations because of the specific circumstances in the European union.

May I add one thing, which was our concern during that negotiation process, but also since that, and I think it is still extremely important issue. And the question is what is the European Union for? What is the fundamental reason why we have this union? And I think I have seen a lot of difficulties now in these circumstances because we want to have this European dimension everywhere every single decision should be in some way or other connected to the European Union policies. And that is a fundamental mistake. That is a fundamental mistake. We need the European Union that was the original idea when we joined the Union, we needed the European Union because national decision-making had limits. If you look at environmental issues, trade issues, certain fundamental economic issues, or security issues, it is easy to understand that in present circumstances, in the present world, already in the world as it was in the early 1990s, it was impossible to imagine that individual countries, even big countries are able to work alone. We need each other. But only in those issues, which are outside our sovereign unity, and that was the fundamental issue. We decided to give up certain amount of sovereignty in order to get better results in the future. And I think I still believe in that, but the European Union has to concentrate on those issues and try to avoid involving anything else. I think in that way, we can guarantee that there is a public support for the European Union, but now many European politicians and decision-makers are trying to get acceptance for the European Union by expanding its role in every single area possible. We have made mistakes, and I think that is one reason why populist cry against the European Union is so strong.

Another example of things above national level are the technological developments that are happening and everything from digital single markets to all other developments.

Matilda af Hällström

I'll give the floor to Mr. Yáñez-Barnuevo, and there is another small question to you, so I will put them together. So, the previous question about the autonomous areas, which was from Hasan Akintug, and then this one is from Peter Stadius.

He writes, I understand your comments, that there were almost no objections to the EC/EU in the 1980s, contrary to the opinions on NATO. Is the situation still the same today? Please.

Juan Antonio Yáñez-Barnuevo

I will try to go one by one, first on regional issues in Spain. As you probably know, since our democratic Constitution of 1978 there are 17 autonomous regions in Spain, including the Basque Country and Catalonia, and quite a number of others, and all of them in one way or the other made known their specific needs or requirements in the negotiation and they were taken into account by the national government in Brussels.

Curiously enough, none of those two regions mentioned posed specific problems. The main problem in a way was the Canary Islands. Canary Islands, as you know, is separated from the continent by a certain distance. So, it has these many specifics in terms of tax regime, in terms of assistance from the national government, special trade arrangements, etc.

So, we had to negotiate with the European Commission a specific protocol to the treaty of accession in order to safeguard, many of those specificities of the Canary Islands, which was included in a package that the European Community at the time and now European Union has for peripheral regions. Maybe, you have some other examples. The French also have in other areas and the Portuguese and several other member countries.

At that time, the main problem with the Basque Country was not in the negotiation, but the question of terrorism. Well, that fortunately has been surmounted by, on the one hand, the action of the Spanish security services and the courts in fighting those criminal activities. Second, better cooperation from France and other countries as well, basically France and third, it has to be said, because there was a Spanish government or several successive Spanish governments of different colors which engaged in a sort of a dialogue with the political arm of that terrorist group. And finally, some kind of arrangement could be found and those people now are actively participating in the political life at the local level, at the regional level and at national level. And in fact, there are representatives of that section of the Basque people in the national parliament and they now support the present government. So, this has been surmounted by the rule of law, by international cooperation and by dialogue.

I would like to stress that the situation concerning Catalonia is very different from the one concerning Scotland. Scotland would like to remain in the European Union once the United Kingdom has left. This is not possible, but they aspire to do so. This is a question within the United Kingdom. A part of the Scottish people aspire someday to obtain independence and then join the European Union as an independent country. On the other hand, a part of the Catalonian people would like also to be independent, but then they will have to leave the EEC. If they are independent, they have to leave the European Union. Catalonia can be in the European Union only as a part of Spain. And I must say that the Spanish regions are very active, we have many diplomats, experts, professional, etc. working in the European Union or in Spain with regard to the European Union. And of course, each of those regions has a small representation in Brussels to defend their own interests. And they work together with Spanish representation in Brussels.

This is how it should be, and we hope that it continues that way. The other question, please remind me, I have forgotten, the other question, which was?

Matilda af Hällström

It was about the support or the lack of support or objections towards the EC/EU in the 1980s, contrary to their opinions on NATO. And is this still the same situation today?

Juan Antonio Yáñez-Barnuevo

Sorry for having forgotten. At the beginning there was, as I said, unanimity consensus in the political spectrum. And that lasted until the financial and economic crisis, starting in 2008 in the US and then hitting Europe and particularly Southern Europe in many ways, not just the economic crisis, with unemployment, etc., but especially the strict austerity policies that were, let's say, imposed by Brussels and by Frankfurt especially from 2010 onwards, had a very negative impact in Spain, and I think also in other countries in Southern Europe, Greece Portugal, etc., Italy as well. So, from around 2014, 2015, we had the rise of two populist parties to the extreme right, or to the right of the right, and the other to the left of the left which are critical of European policies. None of them says that they would like to leave the European Union or even to leave the Eurozone. But they are very critical of the European economic model for one reason or the other. The right, because they would like to return to the national state of doing intervention by national state, and to the left because they want a strong intervention by the state, but another, different kind. For now, none of them can aspire to lead the government, I hope they will never lead, but it is true that the left wing of the left government is pushing for some stronger position, especially regarding social policies. And the present government is committed to promote stronger social policies within the bounds allowed by the European treaties and institutions, and that is it.

But certainly, we have to have in mind that now there is not the same kind of social or political unanimity that used to be for the first 15 years of Spain's belonging to the European Union.

Mats Hellström

Well, on the Åland Islands, certainly there was a good solution that was made together, but there were also some suspicions from Stockholm, from some political leaders in Åland, who very informally asked the Swedish government or representatives in the Swedish government to sort of give our view on how the negotiations were going. So, it is a small comment on that, but that certainly was a good solution and the Finnish government made it well, of course.

And then on the question of the scope of the European Union. It is now very often said that it is very strong lack of success when it comes to immigration and migration. That is true, of course, but don't blame the Union because the member States after Maastricht were very keen on keeping hold to the immigration policies at home. You had the so-called third pillar where the commission have less to say much less to establish rules and other things.

Now I think most politicians in many European countries, understand that we have to involve the European Union much more with immigration and migration policies. It has been a failure of the member states who did not want European policies in this theme.

Johan Strang

And Mr. Esko Aho, you wanted to comment, were you aware, I do not know whether your commentary relates to this informal delegation that went from the Åland Islands to Stockholm, were you aware of that?

Esko Aho

I have to say that those local governments in Åland Islands they have been very clever in taking care of their interests, in all circumstances. I remember I was a member of the Nordic Council for several years and they had really skills and talents to take care of their interests.

But I wanted to say one thing, when looking at the European Union today, and these challenges mentioned before related with austerity public support, need for additional social issues on the agenda. I think they are all closely linked to the fact that the common currency was not that kind of success story like expected.

And again, I think it was a fundamental strategic mistake made when decision making was based on the idea that first we will have a common currency and then there is going to be convergence. And these convergence criteria were based on that idea, that you can introduce common currency and then you have criteria so that every country is able to have roughly similar economic development and they are able to meet the criteria set together.

I am afraid this has not worked and it is difficult to get it working in the future as well because the common currency could work well if, and when you have convergence and then you will be able to move to common currency and I am afraid this crises is going to be continued. We are going to have a lot of political challenges inside Europe because of that.

Mats mentioned also this immigration issue, which is another difficult issue. But I think this common currency issue is fundamental and I do not know what to do. It is very difficult to make any major improvements in the system now.

Johan Strang

Thank you. Time is flying and we only have five minutes left. So, I would like to go around all speakers, all witnesses can have one minute, not much more than that, there are still some kind of lessons from the past or lessons from their own perspectives that could perhaps be applied to the present day and future scenarios?

Mats Hellström

I am surprised that it took one hour and 50 minutes roughly before Brexit was mentioned, but that is only one of the challenges that we have now. But I think it is significant in the sense that both in the eighties and nineties the European Union seemed to be, or European cooperation seemed to be the answer to some questions or to challenges.

Matilda af Hällström

Is the European Union still the answer and what is the question to which it is the answer? And I think that some of you have already answered that, but really briefly and simply in one minute, please. Should we start with Yáñez-Barnuevo, please?

Juan Antonio Yáñez-Barnuevo

It is a tall order in one minute, but just to say that for the whole period that Spain has belonged to the European Union we have always tried to be true to that commitment and to join every step of the European integration, Single European Act, Maastricht, etc. We introduced, for instance, the idea of a European citizenship and the mechanism for cohesion, for the social and territorial cohesion in Europe. And then successive steps, Schengen treaty, also the Eurozone. We agree that it is difficult to say whether we can go forward as easily as in the past, for reasons that are our own, and also for reasons having to do with the convergence, as it was mentioned, of the whole, but certainly the majority of the people and the political class in Spain and also the economic leaders and social leaders are in favor of continued European commitment of Spain. And I think there's also that case in Portugal.

And I am glad that it was mentioned that with the 2020 pandemics, the reaction of the European Union has been very different, almost the opposite of what it was in the financial and economic crisis of 10 or 12 years ago. And that is a good thing. It is a good prospect where it is now incumbent upon us, also nationally, not only at the European level, to be true to that and to respond to that and to do it well, this is our responsibility now.

Matilda af Hällström

Thank you.

Antonio Yáñez-Barnuevo
Thank you.

Matilda af Hällström
And then over to Sweden, Mats Hellström.

Mats Hellström
Well, one lesson learned, I think is that you should never underestimate the everyday work or the cooperation. One example during the unwanted pause in the Council work after the negative referendums in Netherlands and France, when the Council did not function, the amount of directors did not go down, thanks to the extra acting commissioner work, never underestimate them.

And from now on, for example, with a new, interesting investment agreement with China, the Commission will again be very important together of course, with the EU external action service and with the Lisbon treaty having been made in late 2000, 2009 also. The role of the European Union is much stronger than before, and we have to also relate to that.

Matilda af Hällström
Thank you. The role of everyday cooperation, what would you like to add Esko?

Esko Aho
I think the foundation for the strength of the European Union and the power of the European Union is the same as with all countries in the world. It is based on science, technology and economy. And if this foundation is good, we can succeed. We can do fantastic things. If it is not working, we are going to be in many kinds of crisis and I am afraid, we have made fundamental mistakes. We have not been able to move ahead in creating a common market for two fundamental technological areas, which are going to be decisive for the future of Europe. One is digital and other is bio, digital and bio. And now finally, when we have resources, huge resources to be used because of this pandemic, why do not we use

these resources in order to get Europe performing much, much better in these two areas? If we are going to succeed in that I am optimistic. If we are going to fail this, I think Europe has difficulties to keep the position that it has today.

Matilda af Hällström
Thank you very much. International cooperation tends to move forward and take great leaps in times of crisis. So, with this, we can conclude our seminar and I thank our three distinguished guests very much for their contribution today. Thank you all, who have helped us for arranging this seminar, Tiedekulma and for the financial support from Nordforsk and from the Academy of Finland.

So, thank you very much. And of course, a big thank you to everyone who has followed this online, on the stream.

Johan Strang
Absolutely.

Matilda af Hällström
This is for you that we made this. Thank you.

Eskho Aho
Thank you.

Mats Hellström
Thank you.

Juan Antonio Yáñez-Barnuevo
Thank you very much. I enjoyed it.

References

Andry, Aurélie, *Social Europe. The Road Not Taken. The Left and European Integration in the long 1970s* (Oxford: Oxford University Press, 2022).

Cavallaro, Maria Elena & Muñoz Sánchez, Antonio, "Relações Portugal-Espanha," in Alice Cunha (ed.), *Os Capítulos da Adesão* (Lisbon: Assembleia da República, 2017), pp. 397–410.

D'Ottavio, Gabriele, "Disenchantment and new heuristic challenges in European Integration history," *Contemporanea. Rivista di Storia dell '800 e dell '900*, Vol. 23, No. 1 (2020), pp. 99–132.

Gilbert, Mark, "Narrating the Process: Questioning the Progressive Story of European Integration," *Journal of Common Market Studies*, Vol. 46, No. 3 (2008), pp. 641–662.

Hansen, Peo & Jonsson, Stefan, *Eurafrica. The Untold History of European Integration and Colonialism* (London: Bloomsbury Academic, 2014).

Kaiser, Wolfram & McMahon, Richard (eds), *Transnational actors and Stories of European Integration. Clash of Narratives* (Abingdon and New York: Routledge, 2019).

Kaiser, Wolfram & Varsori, Antonio (eds.), *European Union History: Themes and Debates* (Basingstoke: Palgrave Macmillan, 2010).

Kaiser, Wolfram, "The EU Referenda in Austria, Finland, Sweden and Norway," Unpublished paper, presented at the 4th European Union Studies Association (EUSA) Biennial Conference 1995, May 11–14, 1995.

Krotz, Ulrich, Patel, Kiran Klaus & Romero, Federico (eds), *Europe's Cold War Relations. The EC Towards a Global Role* (London: Bloomsbury, 2019).

Leucht, Brigitte, Seidel, Katja & Warlouzet, Laurent (eds), *Reinventing Europe. The History of the European Union, 1945 to the Present* (London: Bloomsbury, 2023).

Loth, Wilfred, *Experiencing Europe. 50 Years of European Construction. 1957-2007* (Baden Baden: Nomos, 2009).

Moreno Juste, Antonio & Sanz, Carlos (eds), *Spain and Portugal before the Second Enlargement of the European Communities. A Comparative Study (1974-1986)* (Basingstoke: Palgrave Macmillan, forthcoming).

Moreno Juste, Antonio, "El relato europeo de España: de la transición democrática a la gran recesión," *Ayer. Revista de Historia Contemporánea*, Vol. 117, No. 1 (2020), pp. 21–45.

Patel, Kiran Klaus, "Widening and Deepening? Recent Advances in European Integration History," *Neue Politische Literatur*, 64 (2019), pp. 327–357.

Patel, Kiran Klaus, *Project Europe* (Cambridge: Cambridge University Press, 2020).

Strang, Johan (ed.), *Nordic Cooperation. A European Region in Transition* (London: Routledge, 2015).

Uutela, Marjo, "Closer to Germany than Sweden. Finland's way towards the membership application for the EC 1990–1992," *International History Review*, Vol. 42, No. 5 (2020), pp. 1067–1080.

Warlouzet, Laurent, *Governing Europe in a Globalizing World. Neoliberalism and its Alternatives following the 1973 Oil Crisis* (London: Routledge, 2018).

Samtidshistoriska frågor

This series is published by The Institute of Contemporary History (Samtidshistoriska institutet). The series summarizes and discusses important historical events and contemporary issues. Edited transcripts from witness seminars, new research from the university's academic staff as well as conference reports are published as part of the series. Information about the series: https://bibl-app.sh.se/publicationseries/list?id=12

Most of the titles in the series can be downloaded in full text, free of charge, from the Digital Science Archive, DiVA, http://www.diva-portal.se.

Some of the titles in the series have been published in collaboration with CBEES (Center for Baltic and Eastern European Studies) at Södertörn University. Responsible for the work with the publication series is Associate Professor Carl Marklund, carl.marklund@sh.se.

Publication series

1. *Olof Palme i sin tid.* Ed. Kjell Östberg (2001).

2. *Kvinnorörelsen och '68.* Ed. Elisabeth Elgán (2001).

3. *Riv alla murar! Vittnesseminarier om sexliberalismen och om Pocket-tidningen R.* Ed. Lena Lennerhed (2002).

4. *Löntagarfonderna – en missad möjlighet?* Ed. Lars Ekdahl (2002).

5. *Dagens Nyheter: Minnesseminarium över Sven-Erik Larsson. Vittnesseminarium om DN och '68.* Ed. Alf W. Johansson (2003).

6. *Kvinnorna skall göra det! Den kvinnliga medborgarskolan på Fogelstad – som idé, text och historia.* Eds. Ebba Witt Brattström & Lena Lennerhed (2003).

7. *Moderaterna, marknaden och makten – svensk högerpolitik under avregleringens tid, 1976–1991.* Torbjörn Nilsson (2003).

8. *Upprorets estetik. Vittnesseminarier om kulturens politisering under 1960- och 1970-talet.* Ed. Lena Lennerhed (2005).

9. *Revolution på svenska – ett vittnesseminarium om jämställdhetens institutionalisering, politisering och expansion 1972–1976.* Ed. Anja Hirdman (2005).

10. *En högskola av ny typ? Två seminarier kring Södertörns högskolas tillkomst och utveckling.* Eds. Mari Gerdin & Kjell Östberg (2006).

11. *Hur rysk är den svenska kommunismen? Fyra bidrag om kommunism, nationalism och etnicitet.* Eds. Mari Gerdin & Kjell Östberg (2006).

12. *Ropen skalla – daghem åt alla! Vittnesseminarium om daghemskampen på 70-talet.* Eds. Mari Gerdin & Kajsa Ohrlander (2007).

13. *Makten i kanslihuset. Vittnesseminarium 16 maj 2006.* Eds. Emma Isaksson & Torbjörn Nilsson (2007).

14. *Partnerskapslagen – ett vittnesseminarium om partnerskapslagens tillkomst.* Eds. Emma Isaksson & Lena Lennerhed (2007).

15. *Vägar till makten – statsrådens och statssekreterarnas karriärvägar.* Anders Ivarsson Westerberg & Cajsa Niemann (2007).

16. *Sverige och Baltikums frigörelse. Två vittnesseminarier om storpolitik kring Östersjön 1991–1994.* Eds. Thomas Lundén & Torbjörn Nilsson (2008).

17. *Makten och trafiken i Stadshuset. Två vittnesseminarier om Stockholms kommunalpolitik.* Ed. Torbjörn Nilsson (2009).

18. *Norden runt i tvåhundra år. Jämförande studier om liberalism, konservatism och historiska myter.* Torbjörn Nilsson (2010).

19. *1989 med svenska ögon. Vittnesseminarium om Östeuropas omvandling.* Eds. Torbjörn Nilsson & Thomas Lundén (2010).

20. *Statsminister Göran Persson i samtal med Erik Fichtelius (1996–2006).* Ed. Werner Schmidt (2011).

21. *Bortom rösträtten. Politik, kön och medborgarskap i Norden.* Eds. Lenita Freidenwall & Josefin Rönnbäck (2011).

22. *Borgerlig fyrklöver intog Rosenbad – regeringsskiftet 1991.* Eds. Torbjörn Nilsson & Anders Ivarsson Westerberg (2011).

23. *Rivstart för Sverige – Alliansen och maktskiftet 2006.* Eds. Fredrik Eriksson & Anders Ivarsson Westerberg (2012).

24. *Det började i Polen – Sverige och Solidaritet 1980–1981*. Ed. Fredrik Eriksson (2013).

25. *Förnyelse eller förfall? Svenska försvaret efter kalla kriget*. Ed. Fredrik Eriksson (2013).

26. *Staten och granskningssamhället*. Eds. Bengt Jacobsson & Anders Ivarsson Westerberg (2013).

27. *Almedalen – varför är vi här? Så skapades en politikens marknadsplats – Ett vittnesseminarium om Almedalsveckan som politisk arena*. Ed. Kjell Östberg (2013).

28. *Anarkosyndikalismens återkomst i Spanien. SACs samarbete med CNT under övergången från diktatur till demokrati*. Ed. Per Lindblom (2014).

29. *När blev vården marknad? Vittnesseminarium i Almedalen*. Ed. Kristina Abiala (2014).

30. *Brinner "förorten"? Om sociala konflikter i Botkyrka och Huddinge*. Ed. Kristina Abiala (2014).

31. *Sea of Identities: A Century of Baltic and East European Experiences with Nationality, Class, and Gender*. Ed. Norbert Götz (2014).

32. *När räntan gick i taket: Vittnesseminarium om valutakrisen 1992*. Ed. Cecilia Åse (2015).

33. *Nordiskt samarbete i kalla krigets kölvatten. Vittnesseminarium med Uffe Ellemann-Jensen, Mats Hellström och Pär Stenbäck*. Eds. Johan Strang & Norbert Götz (2016).

34. *Solidariteten med Chile 1973–1989*. Eds. Yulia Gradskova & Monica Quirico (2016).

35. *25 år av skolreformer – hur började det? Vittnesseminarium om skolans kommunalisering och friskolereformen*. Ed. Johanna Ringarp (2017).

36. *Levande campus: Utmaningar och möjligheter för Södertörns högskola i den nya regionala stadskärnan i Flemingsberg*. Eds. Johanna Ringarp & Håkan Forsell (2017).

37. *Utbildningsvetenskap: Vittnesseminarium om ett vetenskapsområdes uppkomst, utveckling och samtida utmaningar*. Eds. Anders Burman, Daniel Lövheim & Johanna Ringarp (2018).

38. *Pontus Hultén på Moderna Museet: Vittnesseminarium på Södertörns högskola, 26 april 2017*. Ed. Charlotte Bydler, Andreas Gedin & Johanna Ringarp (2018).

39. *AIDS i Sverige: Hivepidemin och rörelserna.* Eds. Kjell Östberg & Lena Lennerhed (2019).

40. *Romerna och skolplikten: Hot eller möjlighet?* Ed. Håkan Blomqvist (2020).

41. *Sweden in Solidarity, Museums in Exile: The Chilean Resistance Museum in Solidarity with Salvador. Allende and the International Art Exhibition for Palestine.* Ed. Charlotte Bydler (2022).

42. *Kamp mot droger: En bok om Förbundet mot droger.* Kjell Östberg (2019).

43. *North and South: European Social Democracy in the 1970s.* Eds. Alan Granadino, Carl Marklund & Johan Strang (2021).

44. *Recollections of Joining the EU: Iberian and Nordic Experiences.* Eds. Alan Granadino, Peter Stadius & Carl Marklund (2023).

SÖDERTÖRNS HÖGSKOLA | STOCKHOLM
sh.se

AARHUS UNIVERSITY

UNIVERSITY OF HELSINKI
CENS · CENTRE FOR NORDIC STUDIES

NOS-HS
The joint committee for
Nordic research councils in the
humanities and social sciences

www.ingramcontent.com/pod-product-compliance
Lightning Source LLC
LaVergne TN
LVHW041752190726
843493LV00008B/2589